D0744344

animals**animals**

Dogs

by **Steven Otfinoski**

mc **Marshall Cavendish** Benchmark
New York

Thanks to Donald E. Moore III, associate director of animal care at
the Smithsonian Institution's National Zoo, for his expert reading of this manuscript.

Marshall Cavendish Benchmark
99 White Plains Road
Tarrytown, New York 10591-5502
www.marshallcavendish.us

Library of Congress Cataloging-in-Publication Data

Otfinoski, Steven.
Dogs / by Steven Otfinoski.
p. cm. — (Animals animals)
Includes index.
Summary: "Provides comprehensive information on the anatomy, special
skills, habitats, and diet of Dogs"—Provided by publisher.
ISBN 978-0-7614-3970-7
1. Dogs—Juvenile literature. I. Title.
SF426.5.O84 2009
636.7—dc22
2008020902

Photo research by Joan Meisel

Cover photo: Mark Raycroft/Minden

The photographs in this book are used by permission and through the courtesy of:
Alamy: tbkmedia.de, 10; Petra Wegner, 13; Images of Africa Photobank, 18; Mark J. Barrett, 21; Marmaduke St. John, 24;
Visual&Written SL, 27; Linda Freshwaters Arndt, 28; David R. Frazier Photolibrary, Inc., 32; F1online digitale Bildagentur
GmbH, 33; Daniel Dempster Photography, 39. *Animals Animals—Earth Scenes*: Gerard Lacz, 16; Landau, Bill, 22.
Art Directors & Trip: W. Winstanley, 14; *Corbis*: DLILLC, 1; Tom Brakefield, 6; Dale C. Spartas, 34. *drr.net*:
David Rawcliffe, 30; Thomas A. Kelly, 41. *Getty Images*: Cheryl Ertelt, 4; Ken Weaver, 37. *Hachiko & Kojiki Images*: 29.
Minden Pictures: Mark Raycroft, 9; Mitsuaki Iwago, 26. *Peter Arnold Inc.*: Gerard Lacz, 8; Wegner, P., 11.
Photo Researchers, Inc.: Guy Trouillet, 7. *SuperStock*: Hemis.fr, 36.

Editor: Joy Bean
Publisher: Michelle Bisson
Art Director: Anahid Hamparian
Series Designer: Adam Mietlowski

Printed in Malaysia
1 3 5 6 4 2

Contents

1 Man's Best Friend

Do you own a dog? If not, you probably know someone who does. Dogs are loving, loyal, and intelligent animals. What more could you ask for in a pet? Dogs were the first animals trained and tamed by humans and they remain some of our favorites. Whether they are family-loving pets or hardworking companions, dogs are man and woman's best friend.

How did dogs become our closest friends in the animal world? It all began about 14,000 years ago. Wild animals called wolves began to hang around human communities to eat food that the humans threw away.

Many people who have dogs know that they can be trusting, loving, friends.

Over time, the humans tamed and trained some of these wolves. In return for food and a warm fire to live by, the tame wolves guarded the humans' homes from enemies when the humans hunted. These tame wolves eventually became *domestic* dogs.

Dogs today still have traces of the wolf's nature. Have you ever seen a dog turn around three times before it lies down? Wolves do this to flatten grass and make a soft bed for themselves outdoors. Most pet dogs do not sleep in the outdoors, but they have retained this *inherited behavior*.

The domestic dog is an ancestor of the wolf.

If a dog barks at you when you walk by its house, it is just protecting its territory.

When a person or another dog walks by your house, your dog might leap to life and bark madly at the passerby. This is more wolf behavior. Your dog is defending its territory, which includes your house and yard. Wolves live in packs, or small groups, that are led by a male leader. Your dog has a pack, too—you and your family. It has transferred its loyalty from the wolf pack leader to your family members. It will follow your commands just as it would follow its pack leader's. Well, most of the time it will. Every dog has a mind of its own, too.

Species Chart

◆ The Saint Bernard is one of the biggest and heaviest dogs, weighing as much as 200 pounds (90 kilograms). Males are 27.5 inches (70 centimeters) or taller measured at their *withers*, the highest point of their back at the base of the neck. Females are 25 inches (63.5 cm) or taller. The Saint Bernard is an example of a working dog. For centuries, people have used this dog in the Swiss Alps to rescue people caught or lost in the snow. They are powerful dogs with loving personalities.

A Saint Bernard.

A yellow Labrador Retriever.

◆ The Labrador Retriever has been the most popular *breed* of dog in the United States for nearly twenty years. It has a strong build and a short, thick coat of hair. Males are 22.5 to 24.5 inches (37 to 62 cm) tall and females are 21.5 to 23.5 inches (55 to 60 cm) tall. Male Labradors weigh between 65 and 80 pounds (29 and 36 kg) and female labs weigh between 55 and 70 pounds (25 and 32 kg). They have unusually flattened tails. The Labrador Retriever is an example of a hunting dog, although today it is mainly raised to be a family pet.

◆ Poodles are known for their thick, curly topcoats that look beautiful when groomed properly. Standard poodles are more than 15 inches (38 cm) tall, but this breed also comes in miniature and toy sizes. The poodle has a square build. It is solid in color, and can be white, black, or gray. The poodle is an example of a nonsport dog.

A Standard Poodle.

Two Chihuahuas.

◆ The Chihuahua is the smallest dog breed. It stands only 5 inches (13 cm) tall and weighs under 6 pounds (2.7 kg). It has big eyes and a head shaped like an apple. The Chihuahua is a spirited dog, totally devoted to its owner. It is named for the Mexican state where it was first bred. The Chihuahua is an example of a toy dog.

There are more than 150 breeds of dogs. A *purebred* is a dog whose parents belong to the same breed. A *crossbreed* is a dog whose parents are of different breeds. A *mongrel* is a dog whose parents' breeds are unknown.

Although there are many breeds of dogs, nearly all of them share certain characteristics. They all have four legs with paws for feet. Most dogs have tails and two *coats* of fur or hair coverings on their bodies. The outer coat has long guard hairs. These protect the dog's body from rain and snow. The undercoat has short thick hair that keeps the dog warm in cold weather. Most dogs *shed* their hair and grow new hair twice a year. Some dogs, such as Labrador Retrievers, shed year-round.

Each dog paw has four toes and each toe has a toenail or claw. Unlike a cat's claws, dog's claws are not retractable—that is, they cannot pull their claws back into their paws. The bottom of each paw is covered with cushion-like pads that are covered with a tough skin.

Did You Know . . .

The poodle was first developed in Germany as a water dog. Hunters used poodles to retrieve birds. The poodle's name comes from the German word, *pudel,* which means "to splash in the water."

Adult dogs have forty-two teeth. Twelve *incisors* in front are for picking up food. Four large *canine teeth* tear the food and pass it back to twenty-six premolars and molars that grind and crush the food.

A dog cannot retract its claws like a cat can.

When you see a dog panting, it means it is trying to cool itself off.

Dogs have sweat *glands*, but they do not function well. To cool off in hot weather, a dog opens its mouth and pants. This causes water in the dog's mouth to evaporate and helps cool off the dog.

Several of a dog's senses are far sharper than humans' senses. A dog's hearing is extremely keen and it can hear sounds that a human's ears cannot detect. Dogs with pointed ears can rotate their ears in the direction of a sound to pinpoint its exact location. They can also recognize sound patterns. For example, they can distinguish one family member's footsteps from another.

A dog's sense of smell is truly extraordinary. It has about 220 million smell-sensitive cells in its heads. Humans have only five million such cells. When you take a dog for a walk, it often spends much of its time sniffing at everything in its path. Dogs do this to identify objects, plants, other animals and people by their smells. When you give a dog a morsel of food it will always smell the food before eating it. That is because its sense of smell is so much more advanced than its sense of taste. It can identify almost anything

Dogs will sniff each other when they meet for the first time.

it eats by its odor. Have you ever wondered why a dog's nose is always slightly wet? A gland inside the nose secretes fluid. This moisture helps the dog's nose to detect smells.

A dog's strong sense of hearing and smell make up for its eyesight, which is not as good as human eyesight. Dogs are color-blind and have difficulty seeing patterns and forms, but they have better vision than humans at dusk and at night.

A Communicating Carnivore

Dogs are part of a family of animals that are called canidae. These meat-eating animals include wolves, coyotes, foxes, jackals, and wild dogs such as the dingoes of Australia. Unlike most of these animals, however, dogs are actually *omnivores*. This means they eat both plants and animals. Most pet dogs thrive on commercial pet food that can be in the form of dry pellets or wet meat products. Most veterinarians discourage people from regularly feeding dogs table scraps. Some foods are poisonous to dogs, especially chocolate.

This female jackal and her pup are part of the same canid family that dogs are part of.

Dogs communicate with other dogs and humans through sounds and body language. Dogs can make a range of noises including barking, whining, yelping, and growling. A dog's bark can mean different things at different times. When a stranger comes near, its bark is a warning to stay away. When a dog's owner comes home, however, its bark is a sign of joy. A dog playing with another dog barks to show its excitement. A snarling or growling dog is usually showing another dog or enemy that it can not be pushed around and is ready to fight. Dogs whine when they are hurt or frightened.

A dog can express itself through body language, too. It can even show its feelings with its tail. A wagging tail means a dog is happy. A dog holds its tail straight up as a signal to another dog that it is ready to defend itself and fight. When a dog drops its tail between its legs it is usually worried, frightened, or yielding to a more powerful dog.

Sometimes a dog can tell you what it is thinking with its face. A dog may wrinkle

20

When dogs are playing, they may bark or make other noises
to show their excitement.

A dog that has its face tilted to one side is most likely interested in what you are saying.

his forehead to show that it is confused. When a dog tilts its head to one side, it may be saying it is interested in what you are saying.

A dog that wants to play may wag its tail and raise its hindquarters and lower the front of its body into what looks like a bow.

3 A Puppy's Life

Is there anything cuter to watch than *puppies* at play? They jump and roll and tumble over each other, yelping for joy. But at birth, these same puppies are completely helpless.

Puppies are born about nine weeks after two dogs mate. The father is called a *sire* and the mother is called a *dam*. The number of puppies in a *litter* can vary greatly according to the breed of the parents. Most litters have between five and eight puppies, but the litter can be as large as fifteen.

At birth, the puppies can neither see nor hear. Their eyes are sealed shut and so are their ears. They rely on their senses of smell and touch to find their

These newborn puppies snuggle close together to stay warm.

way to one of their mother's *teats*, where they can suck her milk. This is the only food they will eat for about three weeks.

After ten to fifteen days, the puppies' eyes open. Their eyes are usually blue at first and then gradually darken to brown or black. A few breeds, like the

A mother dog may give birth to as many as fifteen puppies at one time. This golden retriever gave birth to just six puppies.

Siberian husky, keep their blue eyes all their lives. By about three weeks, the puppies' ears open and they can hear for the first time. About the same time, they start to grow their first baby teeth, and they can eat solid foods. Each puppy will grow a full set of twenty-eight baby teeth. By the time the puppy is five months old, forty-two adult teeth have replaced these baby teeth.

About the same time, the puppies learn to stand on their little feet. Soon they are scampering around and playing with each other. The mother stops feeding them her milk at about six weeks. This process is called *weaning*. At about eight weeks, the puppies are ready to be adopted by human families. It is important that they start having contact with

Puppies are ready to be adopted when they are eight weeks old.

This seven-month-old basenji puppy is almost full grown.

people at this time. This will ensure that they will form the same kind of emotional bond with humans as they did with their mother and littermates.

The puppy part of a dog's life is brief. By about eight months many puppies are full grown. Some dogs, especially large ones, mature more slowly and stay puppies for up to two years. A dog's life span varies according to its size. Small and medium dogs generally live up to about fifteen years. Large dogs live for an average of about ten years.

4 Adaptable Dogs

Dogs are adaptable animals. For the last 14,000 years they have learned how to live with humans around the world. Most pet dogs live in the same environment as their masters, but their needs vary with breed and size. Toy dogs and small dogs are often content to live mostly indoors and in small spaces. Medium and large dogs, such as a greyhound or a Saint Bernard, need more space and exercise. They need to be walked outdoors at least twice a day on a leash and, if possible, let loose to run and play in a closed yard or a field in the countryside.

Many dogs love to run and jump to release some of their energy.

A dog's personality usually depends on the breed of the dog. For instance, herding dogs such as the Border Collie or a Jack Russell terrier have a lot of energy. This means they may need more exercise than a lower-energy dog like a pug.

Dogs enjoy the company of other dogs. Walking is important because it allows dogs to meet other dogs. Many communities, such as cities where there may not be a lot of green space, have established special dog parks. They are enclosed outdoor spaces meant just for dogs and their owners. Dogs can be unleashed

Dogs and humans get to meet each other at this city dog park.

Dogs need time every day to walk or run outside the house.

and are free to run and play with other dogs. Dog owners can enjoy meeting other dog owners, too.

Most domestic dogs do not have to worry about *predators*. But in areas near forests or other wilderness regions, wild animals can be a threat. Dogs, especially small ones, have been killed by wild animals such as coyotes, wolves, bears, and mountain lions. People who live in areas where these wild animals have been seen should keep a close eye on their pets and not let them roam outside their yard. Pets should be kept indoors at night in order to avoid being stalked by predators at that time.

Did You Know . . .
One out of every three families in the United States has at least one dog.

5 Dogs and People

Dogs and people have been getting along as good friends for a long time. Most of us require nothing more from our "best friends" than a wagging tail and a lot of love. But there are many dogs that do much more to earn their keep and their masters' love. Sporting dogs—including pointers, retrievers, and setters—help hunters find game birds and then fetch or retrieve them. Hounds with their keen sense of smell can also aid hunters.

Dogs help law enforcement agencies to sniff out drugs and other illegal goods that people carry with them into airports and other places. Saint Bernards

This English setter helps hunters find their game birds.

help search for and rescue people in trouble. Alaskan huskies pull sleds carrying people and goods in the frozen northern part of the world. Doberman pinschers guard homes and property against intruders.

These dogs pull a woman on her sled.

This Border Collie herds sheep.

German shepherds and other super-intelligent dogs work as Seeing Eye dogs, guiding blind and visually impaired people. Collies herd animals such as cattle and sheep. Terriers were once used to catch rodents.

Most people treat their dogs well, but some people mistreat and abuse dogs. A mistreated dog may become dangerous to other people. It might attack or bite without warning. It is not the dogs that are bad; it is people who train them to do bad things.

Other people think they are being good to their dogs when they are actually being cruel. Such people allow their dog to mate with another dog and have babies. Because of this, many unwanted dogs are brought into the world each year. Many of these dogs are abandoned to live on the streets, and they become a public nuisance and a health hazard. Many abandoned dogs end up in animal shelters. If nobody adopts these dogs within a certain time period, they are put to sleep and destroyed. Millions of dogs in the United States face this fate each year.

Veterinarians and animal rights organizations strongly recommend that new dog owners have their dogs operated on at an early age to prevent them from having babies. In females, this simple operation is

Did You Know . . .

Terriers got their name from the Latin word *terra* meaning "earth." These "earthdogs" love to dig in the ground to catch *prey* or simply to experience the joy of digging.

38

Stray dogs are often brought to animal shelters, where they hopefully will be adopted into a loving family.

When a dog is cared for properly, it will provide many years of love and affection.

called *spaying*, and in males it is called *neutering*. The operation not only helps control the dog population but also benefits the dog. He or she stays calmer, less aggressive, and often healthier in old age than dogs without the operation. All these things make for a better family pet.

Keeping a dog is a big responsibility. It requires patience, love, and hard work. But what you get in return is a friend for life.

Glossary

breed—A specific type of animal within a given species.

canine teeth—Four pointed teeth used to tear food.

coats—Layers of fur or hair that cover an animal's body.

crossbreed—The offspring of two animals of different breeds or varieties.

dam—A mother dog.

domestic—Suitable for living and working with humans.

glands—Organs that produce chemicals in the body.

incisors—Front teeth that animals use to pick up and cut food.

inherited behavior—Behavior that is not learned but is passed down from one animal to another.

litter—A group of animals that a mother gives birth to at one time.

mongrel—A dog whose parents' breed or breeds is unknown.

neutering—Operating on a male animal so that it cannot reproduce.

omnivores—Animals that eat both plants and meat.

predator—An animal that preys on and eats other animals.

prey—An animal that is hunted and eaten by other animals.

puppies—Dogs under twelve months of age.

purebred—A dog whose parents belong to the same unmixed breed.

shed—To lose dead hair or fur.

sire—A father dog.

spaying—Operating on a female animal so it cannot reproduce.

teats—The parts of the breasts of female mammals that babies suck on to get milk.

veterinarian—A doctor who cares for animals.

weaning—Stopping the feeding of mother's milk to a young animal.

withers—The highest point of an animal's back at the base of its neck.

Find Out More

Books

American Kennel Club. *The Complete Dog Book for Kids*. New York: Howell Book House, 2008.

Hart, Joyce. *Big Dogs* (Great Pets). New York: Marshall Cavendish, 2008.

Hart, Joyce. *Small Dogs*. (Great Pets). New York: Marshall Cavendish, 2009.

Jenkins, Steve. *Dogs and Cats*. Boston: Houghlin Mifflin, 2007.

Mehus-Roe, Kristin. *Dogs for Kids*: *Everything You Need to Know About Dogs*. Irvine, CA: BowTie Press, 2007.

Web Sites

A Kid's Guide To Dog Care
http://www.loveyourdog.com/

Dog Breed Information
http://www.dogluvers.com

Dog Care, Photos, and More
http://www.healthypet.com

Index

Page numbers for illustrations are in **boldface**.

About the Author

Steven Otfinoski is the author of numerous books about animals. He has written *Koalas, Sea Horses, Alligators,* and *Hummingbirds* in the Animals Animals series. Steve lives in Connecticut with his wife, a high school teacher and editor.